THERE IS NOTHING BETWEEN THESE ATOMS

poems

CHERONE BELLINFANTIE

Copyright © 2022 by Cherone Bellinfantie

All rights Reserved
Illustrations by Cherone Bellinfantie
Book design by David Provolo
First paperback edition 2022

ISBN: 979-8-9850778-0-3
Published by Blue Horn Publishing

For the women
who have touched my life
and know the strength that comes with suffering

CONTENTS

CARBON

How Our Bodies Betray Us 8
Souls Tied to the Memory of Murmurs 9
The Wheel of Life 10
Ghosted 12
The Dislocated Body 14
A Woman's Burden 16
Homecoming 18
Baker Act 20

ETHER

Meditation 24
The Goddess Reigns Supreme 25
Drishti 26
I Forget Myself in the Evening 28
The Passing Cloud 29
There Is Nothing Between These Atoms . . 30

From a hole you came;
To the whole you will return

CARBON

How Our Bodies Betray Us

Beneath my school uniform,
new breasts.
The other girls' chests
lie flat and obedient.
Mine lies about my age.

Souls Tied to the Memory of Murmurs

Sunlight filters through
  the warped window,
your Nikes slouch
against the cold brick wall
under a film of dust

  the prison bed waits for us
in the middle of the room.

Laid open to you,
  you sneak beneath
my thirsty skin,
your purple lips on mine,
commemorating moans.

  Between my legs, you spin ropes.
Your flesh has become my own.

The Wheel of Life

Tragic circumstances produce damaged materials
and require you to trust the broken pieces.
The tarnished collection copies the past
and you are left with overdue regrets.

Please
is a word you pray.

The universe will charge you
with the quality of your actions
and your soul may be bent
or torn in the process
like a piece of borrowed card.

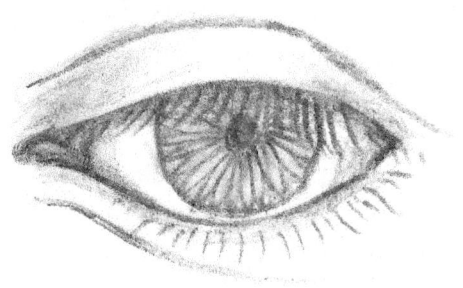

Ghosted

You appear to me in dreams.
I wake up to what I lost,
keep you in a special box
called Maybe.

I knew the games you played
and stayed to play them anyway
hoping you were more
than just your hunger.

You once said
no-one can help but love
someone who loves them.
Now I see it was a test.

I watched you saunter from my doorstep,
words locked inside my throat
like a sparrow
too scared to sing.

You brought me gifts without warning,
then carved a chasm in my chest
with your distance.
My insides twist
when I think of your hand holding mine,
I scrape my mind for signs I missed.

The final memory
of the sweet sweat on your t-shirt
folded on my bed
like a token of goodbye —

you want me to remember
a specter
suspended in this glass heart
that no longer trusts a smile.

The Dislocated Body

Her body is left in a dark corner
with blood
            and the memory of a virgin
                    torn limb from limb
no sponge can scrub off the sin

something was taken
and replaced
            with a black hole,
                  food crammed into the opening
she crouches over a porcelain bowl

                the dead moving
through her painted lips
            dripping the dross
of a stranger
      onto the frigid bathroom floor.

Her body is a dark corner
of secrets and shadows
                      she moves through her life

     like smoke

                smothering the innocent

choking on the shame.

A Woman's Burden

I decided to switch off
my love, said it was for the best,
forced a smile through that crowded bar
and sucked down a rum instead.

Rigid in the waiting room.
Outside, protesters marched and screamed.
All the blank-faced women sitting,
kept their eyes on the tv.

The doctor prescribed a drug
to make my problem go away.
He didn't write a warning for
how long the pain would stay.

I held the pain between my teeth,
swallowed all the pills instead.
I numbed my body and my mind
and said it was for the best.

Homecoming

1.

Dark house, no plants,
death waiting in your fragile arms.
You lie in an alien bed
crowding the room where your laughter
once boomed into every corner.

Dead legs lie
where my mother used to be.
Your golden skin ashy
like the cracked concrete steps
leading to the front door;
thorns claw the window frame.

I beg for you
to come outside and you smile
as if you have so many days.
I swallow my scream
and the unspoken words —
your life is not just for me.

My child-self cleaves
to the warm folds of your flesh
expanding and collapsing
in your nightdress, surrendering
to the last time to smell your skin.

2.

Once I belonged
to a part of you, cocooned
in the blanket of your womb
feeding on the force of your intention
knitted between your bones
and the history of souls.

Landmark for love.
Now, I cannot call the house a home.
Nowhere for me to belong
but the breeze of your spirit
always with me.

Baker Act

Strapped man packs adult attacked
by brain into back of van.
Adult hand grasped, clasped.
Mama denied bye-bye to baby
cradled in her partner's arms.
Crazy lady

        accustomed to aggravation.
        At anterior to asylum
        wardens want assistance
        around altercation.
        Madam granted no absolution,
        forced to sign her autograph.

Woman pads along a tacky mat
between halls of sanguine splashes
all administrating ladies
avoid glancing, gaping
assuming hazard to her madness.

Mama's hands slam chairs
against pistachio walls and glass.
More wardens are called
assuming woman
dangerous.

    Raw women appear in alcoves
    as Mama bawls in a ball
    accosted to absorb
    the sedation medication
    and be
    patient.

ETHER

Meditation

Go into that dark place,
that cave within your psyche
where every chanted word
becomes a cipher in your mind,
piercing your afflictions.
Lie dormant with emotion
clouding your inner vision,
see that darkness can be bliss,
where you are,
between the body and the breath.

The Goddess Reigns Supreme

I will invoke Isis
when illusions irritate my worth.
The iridescence of my inside
will illuminate my longing
and lift me up
with strong legs.
Lonely lips will whisper
words of wisdom
and wonderful love.
I will be a wife to myself
and wreak lightning on wastelands,
inspiring lavender to grow
from weathered rocks
and withering leaves.
Light will linger
from my luminescence.

Drishti

these eyes focus on the space before me

time evaporates into silence

mind anatomized in stillness

shines on every chimera

posed as understanding

my vision reframed

in this moment

where it is

only

me

I Forget Myself in the Evening

looking onto the vista of the setting sun
glinting on a sea of sapphire, celadon

waves crashing, vanishing into a web of foam
my every inhalation is the undertow

dragging hazy rainbows over rocks and skeleton
buried beneath saffron sand striations

sweeping softly over naked fingers and toes
sinking deeper into earth as the waves move close

The Passing Cloud

A pink heart puffs across sky.
Glowing vapors stretch thin.
Nimbostratus looms behind trees.
Sun softens back across horizon.

Mind-molded shapes transform
in the air then slowly drift away.
Canopies sketched in the twilight,
like models of thick, wet clay.

Powdery chiffon-veiled roof
shifts quietly beyond the beyond.
Wisps sheath blinking planes,
flying above shimmering ponds.

There Is Nothing Between These Atoms

We are scattered frequencies of light,
erupting from the dark matter of Mind.
Spirals of time built by the Most High,
cradle our spirits between earth and sky.

Quarks form planets and nebulae,
transform energy and never die.
Aimless atoms, charged and magnetized,
coalesce in carbon and strategize.

Out of the One we all emanate,
reflecting the divine original state,
blessed with the power of mercy and grace,
miracles made in untouchable space.

An invisible tongue heard from within,
speaks softly to guide us with intuition.
Watching with eyes that can never be seen,
we are the God-Self we have always been.

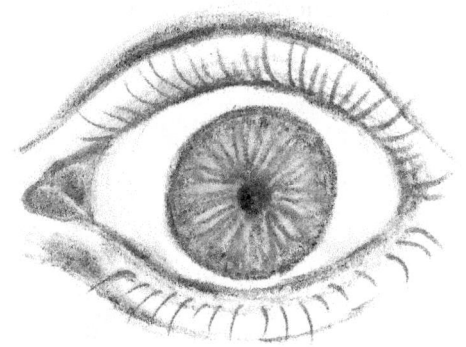

To find more art and writing by
Cherone Bellinfantie
visit her website at
www.cheronebellinfantie.com

www.ingramcontent.com/pod-product-compliance
Lightning Source LLC
Chambersburg PA
CBHW060622070426
42449CB00042B/2466